THE MONUMENT

THE MONUMENT

MARK STRAND

THE ECCO PRESS | NEW YORK

First published by The Ecco Press in 1978
1 West 30th Street, New York, N.Y. 10001
Published simultaneously in Canada by
Penguin Books Canada Ltd.
Printed in the United States of America
The Ecco Press logo by Ahmed Yacoubi
Designed by Cynthia Krupat
The publication of this book is partially supported
by a grant from The National Endowment for the Arts.

Library of Congress Cataloging in Publication Data
Strand, Mark, 1934–
The monument.   /   I. Title.
PS3569.T69M6   /   818'.5'407   /   77–12290
ISBN 0–912–94650–4

To the Translator of

THE MONUMENT

in the future

———

"*Siste Viator*"

THE MONUMENT

Let me introduce myself. I am . . . and so on and so forth. Now you know more about me than I know about you.

1

2 | *I am setting out from the meeting with what I am, with what I now begin to be, my descendant and my ancestor, my father and my son, my unlike likeness.*

Though I am reaching over hundreds of years as if they did not exist, imagining you at this moment trying to imagine me, and proving finally that imagination accomplishes more than history, you know me better than I know you. Maybe my voice is dim as it reaches over so many years, so many that they seem one long blur erased and joined by events and lives that become one event, one life; even so, my voice is sufficient to make The Monument out of this moment.

And just as there are areas of our soul which flower and give fruit only beneath the gaze of some spirit come from the eternal region to which they belong in time, just so, when that gaze is hidden from us by absence, these areas long for that magical gaze like the earth longing for the sun so that it may give out flowering plants and fruit.

Shine alone, shine nakedly, shine like bronze,
that reflects neither my face nor any inner part
of my being, shine like fire, that mirrors nothing.

Why have I chosen this way to continue myself under your continuing gaze? I might have had my likeness carved in stone, but it is not my image that I want you to have, nor my life, nor the life around me, only this document. What I include of myself is unreal and distracting. Only this luminous moment has life, this instant in which we both write, this flash of voice.

4 *Look in thy glass, and tell the face thou viewest*
Now is the time that face should form another . . .

Many would have thought it an Happiness to have had
their lot of Life in some notable Conjunctures of Ages
past; but the uncertainty of future Times hath tempted
few to make a part in Ages to come.

And the secret of human life, the universal secret, the
root secret from which all other secrets spring, is the
longing for more life, the furious and insatiable desire to
be everything else without ever ceasing to be ourselves,
to take possession of the entire universe without letting
the universe take possession of us and absorb us; it is the
desire to be someone else without ceasing to be myself,
and continue being myself at the same time I am some-
one else. . . .

It is a struggle to believe I am writing to someone else,
to you, when I imagine the spectral conditions of your
existence. This work has allowed you to exist, yet this
work exists because you are translating it. Am I wrong?
It must be early morning as you write. You sit in a large,
barely furnished room with one window from which you
can see a gray body of water on which several black ducks
are asleep. How still the world is so many years from
now. How few people there are. They never leave town,
never visit the ruins of the great city.

Or let me put it this way. You must imagine that you are the author of this work, that the wind is blowing from the northeast, bringing rain that slaps and spatters against your windows. You must imagine the ocean's swash and backwash sounding hushed and muffled. Imagine a long room with a light at one end, illuminating a desk, a chair, papers. Imagine someone is in the chair. Imagine he is you; it is long ago and you are dressed in the absurd clothes of the time. You must imagine yourself asking the question: which of us has sought the other?

6 *I have no rest from myself. I feel as though I am devouring my whole life. . . .*

O my soul, I gave you all, and I have emptied all my hands to you; and now—now you say to me, smiling and full of melancholy, "Which of us has to be thankful? Should not the giver be thankful that the receiver received? Is not giving a need? Is not receiving a mercy?"

All voice is but echo caught from a soundless voice.

In what language do I live? I live in none. I live in you. It is your voice that I begin to hear and it has no language. I hear the motions of a spirit and the sound of what is secret becomes, for me, a voice that is your voice speaking in my ear. It is a misery unheard of to know the secret has no name, no language I can learn.

O if you knew! If you knew! How it has been. How the ladies of the house would talk softly in the moonlight under the orange trees of the courtyard, impressing upon me the sweetness of their voices and something mysterious in the quietude of their lives. O the heaviness of that air, the perfume of jasmine, pale lights against the stones of the courtyard walls. Monument! Monument! How will you ever know!

8 | *Then do thy office, Muse; I teach thee how*
To make him seem, long hence, as he shows now.

Through you I shall be born again; myself again and again; myself without others; myself with a tomb; myself beyond death. I imagine you taking my name; I imagine you saying "myself myself" again and again. And suddenly there will be no blue sky or sun or shape of anything without that simple utterance.

Between you and the shapes you take
When the crust of shape has been destroyed.

You as you are? You are yourself.

It has been necessary to submit to vacancy in order to begin again, to clear ground, to make space. I can allow nothing to be received. Therein lies my triumph *and* my mediocrity. Nothing is the destiny of everyone, it is our commonness made dumb. I am passing it on. The Monument is a void, artless and everlasting. What I was I am no longer. I speak for nothing, the nothing that I am, the nothing that is this work. And you shall perpetuate me not in the name of what I was, but in the name of what I am.

10 Perhaps there is no monument and this is invisible writing that has appeared in fate's corridor; you are no mere translator but an interpreter-angel.

I begin to sense your impatience. It is hard for you to believe that I am what you were. It is a barren past that I represent—one that would have you be its sole guardian. But consider how often we are given to invent ourselves; maybe once, but even so we say we are another, another entirely similar.

12 Stories are told of people who die and after a moment come back to life, telling of a radiance and deep calm they experienced. I too died once but said nothing until this moment, not wishing to upset my friends or to allow my enemies jokes about whether I was really alive to begin with. It happened a couple of years ago in March or April. I was having coffee. I know I was dead just a few minutes because the coffee was still warm when I came back. I saw no light, felt no radiance. I saw my life flash before me as a succession of meals and I felt full. This feeling was to give way to an image of waste. How much would be lost! A box placed underground with me inside would never be right. And then I thought of The Monument. It was this promise of adequate memorial that brought me back to life, to my room and my coffee.

Stars denote places where The Monument has been re-ported.

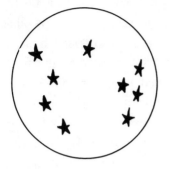

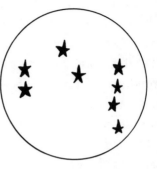

Eastern Hemisphere   Western Hemisphere

14 It may be wise at this time to get down to practical matters, to make suggestions that will ease your task. There are words that I use, words used often in the poetry of my day, which should not constrain you. It is possible that they will not exist in your time or in your language. In either case, find words for which you yourself have a fondness. If this is difficult, then I suggest you use one word to cover the many. The objects you see from where you sit may be "anything." "Anything" may be "nothing," depending on what your feeling is. If "nothing" conveys the wrong idea, use "something." By all means, use "something" if you agree with the poet who shrieks, "There is not nothing, no, no, never nothing."

The certainty of death is attended by uncertainties, in time, manner, places. The variety of Monuments hath often obscured true graves: and Cenotaphs confounded Sepulchres.

The true Monument must survive, must stand by itself despite the possible survival of false monuments. Do not be taken in by structures that call themselves The Monument and look like this:

THE MONUMENT

During the night
a storm broke,
striking the monument,
sending it down,
stone and green
pieces of bronze,
onto the lawn.
Now it lies
among shrubs
and torn limbs
of trees.   You scrape
the pieces clean,
cracks and channels
made by rain, you scrub
away the scars, stains,
names painted
on the pedestal.
When you are done,
nothing about
the monument

will look the same.
The cape will gleam,
curls of hair
will seem to swirl
in the moonlight
or spill
in the bright sun.
No wind will scream
under the arms or chin;
all signs and syllables
of pain will be
rephrased, and when
you leave the monument's
hard gaze, the cold
violet of its shade,
you will not think
of turning back.
Not even fears
of slow decay,
of fires blazing
at its base
will keep you there.
Before you walk away,
you will drop a list
inside its throat
of what to do in case
it falls again.
Your final say
buried in the monument's
cold shape . . .

Or look like this:

THE MONUMENT

You will see it
in the shade or covered
with a shawl
of sunlight or sheen
of wet gray;
or later, barely
visible while
the night passes
with its silent cargo
of moons and stars.
You will see sleeping
figures at its feet;
you will see
in its bleached eyes
baked by sun,
strafed by rain,
the meanness of
the sky; and in
its barely open mouth
perpetual twilight.
You will see it
when you come
and when you leave,
you will see it
when you do not wish to
and you will never know
whose monument it is
or why it came to you . . .

17 How sad it is to come back to one's work, so much less than the world it masks or echoes or reminds one of. Such dreariness to return to one's singleness, one's simple reductions. Poems have come to seem so little. Even The Monument is little. How it wishes it were something it cannot be—its own perpetual birth instead of its death again and again, each sentence a memorial.

If you want me again look for me under your bootsoles.

Who walks where I am not,
Who remains standing when I die.

The Unmonument is my memorial placed upside down in the earth. This least obtrusive of reminders will disturb no one, being in fact a way of burying my death. The inverse of such a tactic would be the unburial of my life. That is, so long as my monument is underground, my life shall remain above. Friend, you are my collaborator in this venture. How much pleasure it gives me to imagine you standing on the very ground that covers my statue, saying:

From south and east and west and north,
roads coming together have led me
to my secret center . . .

And of course it will be late in the day and you will consider the events of your life from the greatest to the most humble. Again words will come to you:

Now I can forget them. I reach my center . . .
my mirror.
Soon I shall know who I am.

19

Spare my bones the fire,
Let me lie entire,
Underground or in the air,
Whichever, I don't care.

Remember the story of my death? Well, I planned it this far in advance. And I did it for you, so you might understand it as none of the others could. When I leaned back on the cold pillows, staring through the open window at the black velvety sky, pointing, though my hand was on the verge of collapsing, and said in a clear, calm voice, "Look! Look!", I was asking the impossible of those loyal friends who were crowded into that small room. For they looked out the window and, seeing nothing, said almost in unison, "What is it?" And I replied in a tone that soothed and urged at once, "There! There!" In a moment I was dead. That is the famous story of my death told, I believe, for a dozen or so years and then forgotten. It is yours because you have found The Monument. Finding The Monument is what I urged when I said, "Look! Look!"

It is my belief that on a certain day in a person's life the shapes of all the clouds in the sky will for a single moment directly over his head resemble him. It has been the sad lot of almost everyone who has ever lived to miss this spectacle, but it has not been so with me. Today I saw The Monument affirmed in heaven. I sat in a chair and looked up by chance and this is what I saw.

A story is told of a man who lived his life anticipating his moment in the heavens, and each day there were clouds he would lie on his back in front of his house. He did this summer and winter and the only rest he got was on clear days or days completely overcast. Finally, when he was very old, he did see himself in the clouds and died immediately after. They found him up on his platform, his eyes wide open, the look of astonishment still upon them.

21 | *We are truly ourselves only when we coincide with nothing, not even ourselves.*

Where do I come from? Though unimportant and irrelevant to so single-minded a venture as The Monument, I believe if I included a few paragraphs from an abandoned autobiography you would see for yourself that I am justified in leaving my life out of our work.

> I have always said, when speaking of my father's father, Emil, that he died a sudden and tragic death by falling into a giant vat of molten metal. The fact is I know only what my father told me—that he suffered an accident in a steel mill and died. The terseness of my father's explanation (no doubt masking some pain at recalling this stage in his own life) created an impression of mystery and violence in my mind. Since the vat of molten metal was the only image I had of the inside of a steel mill, it actually became for me the sole cause of my grandfather's death. And the horror of it put him in a heroic perspective, a perspective which contributed to my impulse to aggrandize my father. As a small boy I wanted a lineage of heroes. It is significant that I would usually add, as epilogue to the tale of Emil's death, the suggestion that he was now part of a Cleveland skyscraper. There is some primitive irony in this, but also a belief in the ultimate utility of his dying, as though it were not merely an accident but self-sacrifice for the public good. His death has become over the years a myth of origin to which I cling almost unconsciously. I say "almost" because whenever I tell of it I am

aware of the slight distortion I may be guilty of. Nevertheless, I feel a compulsion to tell it the way I originally construed it, regardless of the doubts that have increased over the years, and the young boy in me is satisfied.

Of my father's mother, Ida, I have no image whatever, probably because my father had none either. She died giving birth to him. He weighed fifteen pounds.

22 *. . . he ordered them to dig a grave at once, of the right size, and then collect any pieces of marble that they could find and fetch wood and water for the disposal of the corpse. As they bustled about obediently he muttered through his tears: "Dead! And so great an artist!"*

It is good none of my enemies, friends, or colleagues has seen this, for they would complain of my narcissism as they always seem to, but with—so they would claim—greater cause. They would mistake this modest document as self-centered in the extreme, not only because none of their names appears in it, but because I have omitted to mention my wife or daughter. How mistaken they are. This poor document does not have to do with a self, it dwells on the absence of a self. I—and this pronoun will have to do—have not permitted anything worthwhile or memorable to be part of this communication that strains even to exist in a language other than the one in which it was written. So much is excluded that it could not be a document of self-centeredness. If it is a mirror to anything, it is to the gap between the nothing that was and the nothing that will be. It is a thread of longing that binds past and future. Again, it is everything that history is not.

It is easy to lose oneself in nothing because nothing can interrupt and be unnoticed. Why do I do this?

24 There is a day when the daughters of Necessity sit on their thrones and chant and souls gather to choose the next life they will live. After the despots pick beggary, and the beggars pick wealth, and Orpheus picks swanhood, Agamemnon an eagle, Ajax a lion, and Odysseus the life of quiet obscurity, I come along, pushing my way through the musical animals, and pick one of the lots. Since I had no need to compensate for any previous experience and wandered onto that meadow by chance, I found the lot of another man much like me, which is how I found you. And instead of going to the River of Unmindfulness, I wrote this down.

The most enclosed being generates waves.

Suppose the worst happens and I am still around while you are reading this? Suppose everybody is around? Well, there is the crystal box!

26 | I confess a yearning to make prophetic remarks, to be remembered as someone who was ahead of his time; I would like to be someone about whom future generations would say, as they shifted from foot to foot and stared at the ground, "He knew! He knew!" But I don't know. I know only you, you ahead of my time. I know it is sad, even silly, this longing to say something that will charm or amaze others later on. But one little phrase is all I ask. Friend, say something amazing *for* me. It must be something you take for granted, something meaningless to you, but impossible for me to think of. Say I predicted it. Write it here:

[Translator's note: *Though I wanted to obey the author's request, I could not without violating what I took to be his desire for honesty. I believe he not only wanted it this way, but might have predicted it.*]

I am so glad you discovered me. The treatment I have received is appalling. The army of angry poets coming out to whip The Monument.

28 I have begun to mistrust you, my dear friend, and I am sorry. As I proceed with this work, I sense your wish to make it your own. True, I have, in a way, given it to you but it is precisely this spirit of "giving" that must be preserved. You must not "take" what is not really yours. No doubt I am being silly, my fears reflecting jealousy on my part, but I know you only as you work on this text. Whatever else you are is hidden from me. What I fear is that you will tell people in your day that you made up The Monument, that this is a mock translation, that I am merely a creature of your imagination. I know that I intend this somewhat, but the sweet anonymity and nothingness that I claim as my province *do* cause me pain. As I write I feel that this should not be my memorial, merely, but that it should be passed on in no one's name, not even yours.

It occurs to me that you may be a woman. What then? I suppose I become therefore a woman. If you are a woman, I suggest that you curl up inside the belly of The Monument which is buried horizontally in the ground and eventually let yourself out through the mouth. Thus, I can experience, however belatedly, a birth, your birth, the birth of myself as a woman.

. . . a Poet's mind
Is labour not unworthy of regard.

And what I say unto you, I say unto all, Watch!

Sometimes when I wander in these woods whose prince I am, I hear a voice and I know that I am not alone. Another voice, another monument becoming one; another tomb, another marker made from elements least visible; another voice that says *Watch it closely*. And I do, and there is someone inside. It is the Bishop, who after all was not intended to be seen. It is the Bishop calling and calling.

Such good work as yours should not go unrewarded, so I have written a speech for you, knowing how tired you must be. It should be delivered into the mirror.

Labors of hate! Labors of love! I can't go on working this way, shedding darkness, shucking light, peeling pages. There is no virtue in it. The author is the opposite of a good author, allowing no people in his work, allowing no plot to carry it forward. Where are the good phrases? They're borrowed! It all adds up to greed—his words in my mouth, his time in my time. He longs to be alive, to continue, yet he says he is nobody. Does he have nothing to say? Probably not. Anonymous, his eyes are fixed upon himself. I grow tired of his jabbering, the freight of his words. My greatest hope is his continued anonymity, which is why I bother to finish The Monument.

[Translator's note: *I must say that he has expressed my feeling so adequately that I find myself admiring him for it and hating myself somewhat.*]

32 Flotillas! Floating gardens skimming the sky's blue shell. Great gangs of gang-gangs and galahs. The air has never been so pure, my lungs are two pink sacks of moist down-under light. Friend, The Monument shines in the tabernacle of air, and at night, under the Southern Cross and the silent sparkling bed of stars, it sings. Friend, this is the place to do your monument. Go among the gang-gangs and galahs!

The drift of skeletons under the earth, the shifting of that dark society, those nations of the dead, the unshaping of their bones into dirt, the night of nothing removing them, turning their absences into the small zeros of the stars, it is indeed a grave, invisible workmanship. O Monument, what can be done!

34 They are back, the angry poets. But look! They have come with hammers and little buckets, and they are knocking off pieces of The Monument to study and use in the making of their own small tombs.

First silence, then some humming,
then more silence, then nothing,
then more nothing, then silence,
then more silence, then nothing.

Song of My Other Self: There is no other self.

The Wind's Song: Get out of my way.

The Sky's Song: You're less than a cloud.

The Tree's Song: You're less than a leaf.

The Sea's Song: You're a wave, less than a wave.

The Sun's Song: You're the moon's child.

The Moon's Song: You're no child of mine.

There is a sullen, golden greed in my denials. Yet I wish I were not merely making them up; I wish I could be the lies I tell. This is the truth. Knowledge never helped me sort out anything, and having had no knowledge but of nothing suggests all questions are unanswerable once they are posed. Asking is the act of unresolving, a trope for disclosure.

. . . it is to be remembered, that to raise a Monument is a sober and reflective act; that the inscription which it bears is intended to be permanent and for universal perusal; and that, for this reason, the thoughts and feelings expressed should be permanent also—liberated from that weakness and anguish of sorrow which is in nature transitory, and which with instinctive decency retires from notice. The passions should be subdued, the emotions controlled; strong indeed, but nothing ungovernable or wholly involuntary. Seemliness requires this, and truth requires it also: for how can the Narrator otherwise be trusted?

Julius Scaliger, who in a sleepless Fit of the Gout could make two hundred Verses in a Night, would have but five plain Words upon his Tomb.

Tell me that my ugly tomb, my transcending gesture, my way into the next world, your world, my world made by you, you the future of me, my future, my features translated, tell me that it will improve, that it will seem better for my not giving into what passes for style, that its prose shall never wear a poem's guise at last, tell me that its perpetual prose will become less than itself and hint always at more.

The epic of disbelief
blares oftener and soon . . .

Some will think I wrote this and some will think you
wrote this. The fact is neither of us did. There is a
ghostly third who has taken up residence in this pen,
this pen we hold. Not tangible enough to be described
but easy to put a finger on, it is the text already written,
unwriting itself into the text of promise. It blooms in its
ashes, radiates health in its sickness. It is a new falsity,
electric in its clumsiness, glad in its lies. And it loves
itself as it fears death.

I wonder if my poverty would be more complete without you or whether you complete it, the last straw taken away. Having said such a thing I feel a surge of power, I, a single strand, upright, making translation less and less possible. Beautiful swipes of clarity fall upon me, lights from the luminous bells of heaven. I tell you this robe of harmless flames I wear is no poor man's torn pajamas. There's no poverty here, with or without you. Translate. Translate faster. Brief work, isn't it, this feathery fluke!

40 To be the first of the posthumous poets is to be the oldest. This will make children of the poets of Europe, the dead poets of Europe. There must be something America is first in. Death and post-death meditations! Glory be! A crown on our heads at last! But what is America to you or you to America?

Solemn truths! Lucid inescapable foolishness! None of that for me! To be the salt of Walt, oceanic in osteality! Secure in cenotaph! The hysterical herald of hypogea! The fruit of the tomb! The flute of the tomb! The loot of gloom! The lute of loot! The work of soon, of never and ever! Saver of naught. Naughtiness of severance. Hoot of hiddenness. I give you my graven grave, my wordy ossuary, tell-tale trinket of transcendence, bauble of babble, tower of tripe, trap of tribute, thought-taxi from one day to the next, nougat of nothing, germ of gemini, humble hypogeum!

42 We have come to terms without terms, come round almost to the end. A relief, but only a stage, bare stage, first stage. We have allowed the enormous airs of the future to engulf us—to be sung, to be borne and born. Heirs of ourselves, ourselves heirs, salvos of air. Without weight the future is possible, here without our waiting. I embrace you in this madness, this muscular mouthing of possibles. The enormous airs—the giant cloudsongs that will reign and reign. Friend, they are coming and only we know it. Perhaps we should be silent, tell no one and the airs will pass, pass without knowledge of themselves, never having been termed, tuned in turmoil, termed harmless.

Heavy glory upon us. Hang on. I must praise my brothers and sisters in the lost art, spitting into the wind, beating their heads against the stars, eating their words, putting their feet in their mouths, hating each other, all of them either lovely or fearful.

43

44 I feel nostalgia for poetry and believe The Monument should have some lines like:

> Invisible lords among the stars
> Over the heads of deep astronomers

or:

> The moon sucking the sea, sucking
> The light from our eyes as we sleep

That sort of thing. But it would never do. Too hard to translate out of the original. After the blazing plainness of The Monument's prose it doesn't stand up. And yet, there's a longing that has no voice and wants one, that fears it will die of itself. There are moments that crave memorial as if they were worthy, as if they were history and not merely in it, moments of the bluest sky, of the most intense sun, of the greatest happiness of the least known man or woman, moments that may have gone on for years in the most remote village on earth. They shall exist outside The Monument.

We are the enemies of pastoral violence, lovers of cold; the body recumbent like The Monument is for us the goodest good; heavy allusions to weather are just another load to us. Give us a good cigar, a long ash that we can speculate on. And plenty of smoke. Ho hum. Now give us a glass of Spanish brandy. Give us a blank wall that we might see ourselves more truly and more strange. Now give us the paper, the daily paper on which to write. Now give us the day, this day. Take it away. The space that is left is The Monument.

46 It is the crystal box again. Let it be a sunlit tomb, a clear tumulus. Let us stand by it, by the life it promises. If we bask in its brightness, we shall be saved, we shall grow into the language that calls from the future, The Monument reaching out.

Spin out from your entrails, therefore, my soul, and
let come what may! More empty space, more void . . .

Till the bridge you will need be form'd, till the ductile
*   anchor hold,*
Till the gossamer thread you fling catch somewhere, O
*   my soul.*

Prose is the language of meaning so I suppose I mean what I say. I say what I say because it is prose. And so it is; describing the circle, the naught of my means, I am taking away, subtracting myself from my words. My blank prose travels into the future, its freight the fullness of zero, the circumference of absence. And it misses something, something I remember I wanted. Soon I shall disappear into the well of want, the *lux* of lack.

48 It is the giant of nothingness that rises beyond, that rises beyond beyondness, undiscovered in the vault of the future, in the leap of faith. If there were a limb here, a limb there, on the desert sand, *that* would be something. If on the pedestal these words appeared: "I am The Monument. Should you doubt this, look around you and compare," *that* would be something. But The Monument has no monument. There are no powers that will work for it; earth, sky, and breathing of the common air, all will forget. O most unhappy Monument! The giant of nothingness rising in sleep like the beginning of language, like language being born into the sleeper's future, his dream of himself entering the beyond. O happy Monument! The giant of nothing is taking you with him!

I have no apologies, no words for disbelievers. What do I care if there is nothing sublime in this summery encounter with the void or voided mirror? We go our ways, each without the other, going without a theory of direction, going because we have to. Why make excuses? Friend, tell them I see myself only as happy. Let them say what they will, The Monument will pretend to be dead.

50 | *Here I lie dead, and here I wait for thee:*
        So thou shalt wait
Soon for some other; since all mortals be
        Bound to one fate.

Our Fathers finde their graves in our short memories, and sadly tell us how we may be buried in our Survivors.

Now here I am at the end waiting for you, ahead of my time, ahead of yours. Such irony should be its own reward, but here I am at the end, the letter ended, The Monument concluded, but only briefly; for it must continue, must gather its words and send them off into another future, your future, my future. O poor Monument to offer so little even to those who have made you!

If I were to die now without The Monument, none of my words would remain. How sad it is to think of the hours wasted while this triumph of ease and crudity that has taken so little time should last centuries, towering over the corpses of poems whose lyrical natures flew off like the best intentions. If I were to die now, I would change my name so it might appear that the author of my works were still alive. No I wouldn't. If I were to die now, it would be only a joke, a cruel joke played on fortune. If I were to die now, your greatest work would remain forever undone. My last words would be, "Don't finish it."

. . . Oh, how do I bear to go on living! And how could I bear to die now!

O living always, always dying!
O the burials of me past and present,
O me while I stride ahead, material, visible, imperious as ever;
O me, what I was for years, now dead, (I lament not, I am content;)
O to disengage myself from those corpses of me, which I turn and look at where I cast them,
To pass on, (O living! always living!) and leave the corpses behind.

ACKNOWLEDGMENTS

Sources of the quotations used in The Monument *are listed here by section and in the order in which they appear in each section.*

2 | "The Old Poem" by Octavio Paz. From *Eagle or Sun?*, translated by Eliot Weinberger. Copyright © 1976 by Octavio Paz and Eliot Weinberger. Reprinted by permission of New Directions Publishing Corporation.

3 | "The Secret of Life" by Miguel de Unamuno. From *The Agony of Christianity and Essays on Faith*, translated by Anthony Kerrigan. Copyright © 1974 by Princeton University Press. Volume 5 of *The Selected Works of Miguel de Unamuno*, Bollingen Series LXXXV. Reprinted by permission.

"Nuances of a Theme by Williams" by Wallace Stevens. From *The Collected Poems of Wallace Stevens*. Copyright © 1923, renewed 1951 by Wallace Stevens. Reprinted by permission of Alfred A. Knopf, Inc.

4 | Sonnet Number 3 by William Shakespeare.

"Letter to a Friend" by Sir Thomas Browne. From *The Prose of Sir Thomas Browne*. W. W. Norton and Company, Inc., 1972.

"The Secret of Life" by Miguel de Unamuno.

6 | *The Seagull* by Anton Chekhov.

"*Thus Spoke Zarathustra*" by Friedrich Nietzsche. From *The Portable Nietzsche*, translated by Walter Kaufmann. Copyright © 1954 by The Viking Press, Inc. Reprinted by permission.

"To a Little Girl, One Year Old, in a Ruined Fortress" by Robert Penn Warren. From *Selected Poems 1923–1975*. Copyright © 1955 by Robert Penn Warren. Reprinted by permission of Random House, Inc.

8 | Sonnet Number 101 by William Shakespeare.

9 | "The Man with the Blue Guitar" by Wallace Stevens. From *The Collected Poems of Wallace Stevens*. Copyright © 1936 by Wallace Stevens. Renewed 1964 by Holly Stevens. Reprinted by permission of Alfred A. Knopf, Inc.

15 | "Hydriotaphia or Urne Buriall" by Sir Thomas Browne.

18 | "Song of Myself" by Walt Whitman.

"I Am Not I" by Juan Ramon Jimenez. From *Forty Poems of Juan Ramon Jimenez*, translated by Robert Bly. Copyright © 1967 by The Sixties Press. Reprinted by permission of The Seventies Press.